I0390598

THE REAL ESTATE AGENT'S GUIDE TO PROPERTY MANAGEMENT

❋ ❋ ❋

Introduction

It was about 8am and I just received word that after 3 months of no rent, the tenants in unit B had moved out in the middle of the night and were nowhere to be found. This was not good.

I quickly drove over to the property to inspect the unit. I had my key, so I knocked on the door and turned the handle. It appeared the electricity had been off for a while because the lights weren't coming on and it was very musty inside. As I passed over the threshold at first I thought there was some water dripping onto my head, but there was something strange about this particular water... It only took a second to realize that what was falling on my head from above the door, were live cockroaches! They were in my hair, they were in my clothes, they were everywhere. I was instantly on the front lawn doing a hop, jump and skip frantically brushing myself off. Any neighbors who happened to be observing this were no doubt entertained. I, on the other hand was furious. You see this property was supposedly being handled by a professional management company. But now, due to the management companies lack of oversight, the unit had become (among other things), completely infested with roaches. They were in everything! Between the doors, the walls, the floors, everywhere. When you stepped on the carpet, it looked like the floors were literally moving! Even to this day, that's probably still one of the worst roach infestations I have ever seen. That wasn't the only problem. I found the roof was leaking, mold was growing inside and there was a problem with the main water line that had been neglected as well. None of this had been communicated to me at any point.

Here's what happened. I had purchased a duplex, and hired a management company to handle the leasing. It looked like a great investment at the time. I got a good price on the duplex and there was a strong demand for rentals. With a professional property management company in place handling the leasing and tenants, life was good. Retirement, here we come! Or so I thought....

Soon reality set in. Come to find out, not all property managers are good, and apparently the ones I hired, were especially bad. I had naively assumed that they would look out for me and my property as I had hired them to do. But that was not what they did at all. They put their interests first, earning themselves plenty of fees, but costing me tremendous amounts of time and money.

These managers, were not only ruining my property, but they were going to ruin my reputation as well. It was at that moment, standing there brushing away the last of the roaches that I decided to dedicate myself to learning all I could about property management and to become the best property manager I could be. That was almost 10 years ago now and it has been quite the adventure. It's a continuing journey and I strive to learn and grow everyday when it comes to being a professional property manager. I always try to remember the stress I had as an owner dealing with a management company that did not care one bit, and I promised that I would never let one of my owner clients or one of my tenants get into one of those situations ever again. It was my hope that when I managed a property for an owner they would say thank you. But, in order for that to happen, I would have to work hard at knowing the business and understanding how to be ahead of the game at all times. Property management can catch you sleeping at the wheel if you're not careful. Houses and buildings don't call you and tell you when they are going to break down or have issues. The key to property management is being proactive rather than reactive. It's about having systems in place to manage people and to manage situations.

When I decided that I would dedicate myself to becoming the best property manager I could be, admittedly, it wasn't necessarily because I had a great passion for property management, but because I felt that if the property management company who I hired to handle my rentals could do it, then any idiot could become a property manager! While that's not exactly the case, that is pretty much how I got started. And I'm so glad that I did. It has been tremendously rewarding and I am thankful for all the ways that I have been able to help people over the years. Now more than ever, as I see the renter economy growing and demand for rentals increasing. I know that more and more real estate agents are going to get involved in leasing and management and it's my hope is that you will use this information to hit the ground running with your property management business while also avoiding some of the mistakes that I made early on.

By the time I was getting into property management I already had a number of years experience in residential real estate. I had a broker's license in 2 states, had owned my own small brokerage at one point and had some flipping and investing experience as well.

I was thinking at the time that this knowledge would give me an edge. I quickly learned that property management was a whole different ball game. While there are similarities, property management was definitely different than anything I had done before.

Who is this book for?

If you are a real estate agent looking to add to your skill set and your bottom line with property management, then this book is for you. *The real estate agent's guide to property management* will show agents and managers how to use simple but cutting edge digital marketing ideas and technology based systems to become a more effective property manager or leasing agent.

A question to ask yourself is, why should I provide property management services? There are a number of reasons to get involved in property management. It can be a wonderful compliment to your existing real estate business. With more and more people choosing to rent, it means that the growth opportunity for you to expand your services is huge right now, and the number of people who are looking to rent a home or apartment, will only grow larger. Meaning your opportunity to get involved in the "renter economy," is now.

There are a number of different types of property managers. The most common way to get started, is in residential property management. You can represent tenants by helping people find a home or apartment to rent and you can earn a commission for this. You can also provide ongoing management services to property owners, the details of which we will discuss throughout this book. This is probably the most traditional method of earning income from property management. An agreement will exist between the broker and property owner that will spell out the services provided by the property manager (agent). This is your property management agreement. If your broker or real estate board does not have a property management agreement, find an attorney who specializes in property management and have them help you.

When it comes to representing owners, it's not just investors and businesses who own rental property. In fact, most rental properties are owned by individuals or small investors. There are also a large number of people who have become what is called an, accidental landlord. Which refers to someone who may not have intended to own an investment or rental property but due to financial or some other life circumstances has had to make the decision to rent out the home they own. As these situations become more common, you as the real estate agent, have the ability to help not only investors, but you can also help people who have to rent their home out, but aren't prepared or knowledgable to do so. It is also becoming more common to find yourself with a listing client who says they are considering renting out their house. Not because they are forced to, but because they see it as a good opportunity. Right now there are a tremendous number of homeowners who want to rent their house because it might be a way for them to earn some extra money or cover the mortgage payments. After learning the strategies outlined in this book, you will be better prepared to help your clients make the best decision for them. If they decide to rent it, you can help them. If they decide to sell you can help them with that too. In my career I have focused mainly on property management exclusively. However, I still do a fair number of sales each year, not because I am trying to get listings or do sales, but because I have an existing relationship with the owner of the property already. So when the time comes for them to sell; they call me, because they know me and trust me.

What I've always liked about the property management side of the real estate business is the recurring monthly income. As a real estate agent working on commission only, our paychecks can grow or shrink based on lots of outside factors. But, with property management, there tends to be less volatility once you are up and running. Ensuring steady income as a real estate agent is not always that easy. By choosing to add leasing and management to your skill set, you can create a more reliable monthly income and develop relationships with property owners who will use you as their agent when it's time to sell or buy their rental properties. This approach will provide you with income streams from the management services, and from the commission on the sales as well.

WIth a little knowledge and a little effort you could go out today and land a property management client and start building your monthly management income. As real estate agents we know that our income can sometimes be sporadic and inconsistent when it comes to sales commissions. But there is a way to earn a more steady and reliable income through real estate and that is through performing the services of a property manager to rental property owners. Generally you will receive a percentage of the collected rents. You will also be responsible to handling maintenance calls and rent collection and processing. Property management can be very rewarding if you are prepared and knowledgeable.

The top three reasons to include property management as part of your real estate business are;
1. Create a more reliable income.
2. Build long term relationships with investors and property owners for repeat business.
3. Grow with the new demands of the "Renter Economy".

Clearly there are lots of great reasons to be involved in property management. However, without proper knowledge, you will quickly find out that property management has its own unique set of challenges. As a real estate agent, we don't often receive any training when it comes to leasing and management. So much of what we learn is focused on the sales side of the business. How to work with buyers and how to list homes for sellers. When it comes to property management and leasing, most agents aren't ever introduced to the opportunities. Yet, when asked; it turns out a large percentage of agents would be interested in learning how to manage homes and apartments.

Many agent's don't even realize it's an option, and therefore don't even think of considering it. Which can be an advantage to the agent who is starting now. You will have a skill set and professional knowledge that will only grow in demand.

The Real Estate Agent's Guide to Property Management will provide a foundation of knowledge in property management that will let you hit the ground running on day one.

By the end of this book you will have learned;

- What property management is and the role of the property manager.
- How to market yourself as a property manager using the latest digital and internet marketing techniques.
- Meeting with property owners and investors.
- How to price and prepare rental units for maximum profit.
- How to effectively advertise your rental units.
- Showing and Screening Applicants.
- Choosing to work with affordable housing agencies and assistance programs.
- Completing the lease & moving in.
- Managing for the long term by building relationships.

We will begin by defining what property management is, and the role of the property manager. I will then go over the basics of operations, marketing, and business systems that can help you be more effective as a residential property manager.

One very important skill will be about how to effectively use digital marketing to grow your business. Like any business, you will need to have a steady stream of leads and prospects to fill your pipelines with new clients. Learning digital marketing strategies will help you gain an edge over your competitors.

Having been doing property management full time for close to a decade I have a strong knowledge base in the ins and outs of management. But it has been my deep knowledge of digital marketing that has often given me an edge. If you follow the ideas and strategies that I lay out in this book, you will be able to gain an edge over your competitors as well. Please keep in touch with me and get updates on ideas and strategies for property management and digital marketing for the property management industry at https://PropertyManagementPete.com

In addition to strategies for marketing your services and your properties, we'll discuss meeting with owners and investors of rental properties. These owners can be quite different than meeting with the owners of a home that you list for sale. It will be important for you to have a handle on some basic terminology when it comes to discussing investment property. Owners of rental property tend to be focused on "the numbers" more than anything else. Understanding how to effectively communicate with these owners will be an important factor in your success in property management. We will go into more detail in the chapter *"Meeting with Property Owners and Investors."* Developing, communicating and executing a plan of action to owners will be a cornerstone for your success in property management.

Why listen to me?

Everyone remembers where they were when the 9/11 terrorist attacks hit. It's easy in fact for most of us to remember exactly where we were and what we were doing. I am no different. Except the environment that I was in was rather unique. I was sitting at a rifle range in Ft Leonard Wood, MO - a newly minted recruit of the U.S. Army. I had just entered my Army basic training in late August 2001. When you are in basic training you are not allowed contact with the outside world. There is no television, newspapers or internet. A few weeks into training, it was late morning and we were sitting around waiting to receive instructions from our Drill Sergeants. All of a sudden one of the senior officers approached our platoon and asked us, "who here is from New York City"... the rest is history.

I completed my Army basic training and advanced individual training (AIT), and in 2003 was sent to the middle east for deployment. After I got home in 2004, I came to the decision that I did not want to continue to work for the government and I was going to go to work for myself. I remember reading that many individuals on the Forbes list made their fortunes through real estate. So, I decided to get my real estate license. I went all in at 24 years old and within 2 years I had earned my broker's license and by 26 I owned my own real estate brokerage.

I have been licensed as a real estate broker for over 15 years now. I hold two broker licenses' in two states and have been involved in the leasing and management of hundreds and hundreds of units. I have managed luxury waterfront homes that rent for thousands of dollars per month and I have rented to affordable housing programs where the tenant pays zero. Not to mention everything else in between. Each property type will require different sets of knowledge and skills. I hope to be able to share with you some of the lessons that I have learned along the way, and also to share with you what I know about my two great professional passions; real estate and internet marketing. I had entered the field of real estate with direct intention, but it was the marketing side of things that was brought to me by a twist of fate.

Real Estate & Marketing

I had been working on my new business for about a year when I met a man who would not only become a good friend, but a mentor as well. After we met, I later came to find out that he had been one of the first people to get involved in the internet marketing business in the early 2000's. His business knowledge and skills were unmatched. I was intrigued. In 2007 when I had the opportunity to work for him, I jumped at the idea of being able to learn from his knowledge.

With my friends guidance, and my own passion and interest in learning about internet marketing, I quickly became well versed on the particulars of how search marketing worked. I read and studied all I could and put into use what I was learning. I was soon ranking my websites at the top of the search engines, I was getting a ton of leads and things were cooking.

… We were off to a great start and the future looked bright… or so I thought…

Just 2 years later, we found ourselves in the midst of the Great Recession, and as everyone knows, real estate was hit the hardest. With not enough business experience and not enough capital to keep things going, I ended up closing the brokerage by 2009 and moving out of state to take a job. But it was through my failure that I discovered a lot of valuable business lessons. I learned from my mistakes and was able to start again with a more fresh perspective. Now I have been able to grow my management business by leaps and bounds using the internet marketing knowledge I acquired in the early days. It is something that I have kept up with and continue to study all the time. It is a rapidly changing industry that requires you to keep a constant eye on the developments that could help your business grow. But if you do, you will be rewarded.

In Chapter 2 of this book we will jump right into some of the key basics for marketing your property management business using online and digital strategies. It is the longest chapter in the book because I do my best to share as much valuable marketing information as I can. Unfortunately, it would be impossible to cover everything in just one chapter of a book. But the idea is to provide a strong foundation of the basics that will allow you to get an edge on your competition and start booking property management clients right off the bat.

Becoming a Property Manager

As I mentioned in the introduction of this book, the story of how I decided to become a property manager was after an experience I had with a property management company in 2011. I purchased a duplex and hired a property manager to handle the leasing and operations. To say it was a disaster was an understatement. Even though there were only two units on this property, these guys were so bad at screening tenants that my 2-unit building had 3 evictions inside of a year! They charged huge fees and barely took care of the property. I knew that I could do it better. It was at this point that I set a goal to become the best property manager I could be. I made a promise to myself that I would always put my duties and the needs of my clients first. It has been a long and interesting journey and I have learned many aspects of the business. From different property types to different personality types. If you are involved in property management for any length of time you will come across lots of different situations. My hope in this book is to share with you some of my knowledge and experiences so that you can get started off on the right foot and be the best property manager that you can be! Both for yourself and for your clients.

CHAPTER 1-
DEFINING PROPERTY
MANAGEMENT

* * *

Keep this definition of property management in the back of your mind as the foundation of your actions. There will be something new everyday when it comes to property management. You will have to think on your feet and make decisions in the moment. Having guidelines and principles to fall back on when things seem uncertain is very important. If something doesn't seem right, it probably isn't. Your duties as a manager and agent for the owner are as follows:

1. Achieve the objectives & goals of the property owners
2. Generate income for the owners
3. Preserve and/ increase the value of the investment property.

Ensuring you are putting the needs and objectives of the owner/ client first and foremost is the most important thing to remember as you go about your property management duties. As you perform the management tasks on a daily basis, you will often encounter challenging scenarios. Along with experience and knowledge, guiding principles will help you to make the right decision. There will be pressures from bad tenants who may attempt to take advantage of certain situations. And while we have all heard stories of bad tenants, there are definitely property owners and landlords who will try to take advantage of their position of power, and in certain cases will even break the law to get what they want. You will need to know how to handle these people in a professional manner and avoid from getting involved in anything that could put you or your broker at risk.

One time I dealt with an owner said that he wanted to cancel a lease after he found out the tenant was African American in decent. That was literally his only reason for wanting a cancellation. This person had submitted an application, was qualified financially and had a clean background. She was a ready, willing, and able tenant. We had the authority to complete leases on the owners behalf and it was our responsibility to fill the unit with a qualified renter. So that's what we did. We had strong confidence that this new tenant would be great. She was highly qualified and had a solid rental history. We did not anticipate the reaction of the owner. Usually property owners and investors are thrilled to have such a qualified tenant as a resident. However, apparently this owner was not. I was sitting in my office one afternoon with some associates when he came in and started telling us his thoughts. "I drove by (the house) with the new tenant that you placed last week. I noticed she was black..." He said. "So, what?" I asked.... "I don't want those kind of people in my houses," the owner then told me. Immediately I was on high alert. I couldn't believe what this owner was saying to me. I calmly explained that she was well qualified and there was no reason to believe she wouldn't be a good resident. But, no matter what I told him he didn't seem to hear it. I explained that what he was saying was not only the wrong way to think, but it was also highly illegal. By the end of our discussion we were no further along. The owner was asking me to cancel the lease on the new resident for no reason other than the fact that he didn't like the color of her skin. I explained to him that it was not possible, and that he should forget it and just be thankful that we have such a well qualified tenant.

He wasn't hearing it. He said to me "go figure out a way to cancel that lease, or your fired." - It was at this point I realized there was no way out of this situation and we were not going to be working together anymore after today. So I told him, "If you want to cancel the lease you are going to have to ride over there on your horse, wearing your Klu Klux Klan uniform and cancel the lease yourself". Needless to say, he didn't like this comment and we immediately terminated our agreement right then and there. Not before I warned him however, that if he did attempt to cancel that lease, he would be facing serious legal charges and I would be happy to testify against him.

I explained to the tenant that we would no longer be the management company for the property and if she felt uncomfortable in the home in any way, to contact me right away. I do believe the owner honored the original lease that was in place for that year and I don't know what happened to the tenant from there. I never heard any more about it. But it is a strong reminder that there are people who are going to try to take advantage of a situation and do the wrong thing. You are the professional and it is your responsibility to know and understand the landlord/tenant laws in your state and at the federal level so that you can effectively do your job as a property manager.

Throughout this book we will cover the various "red flags" that potential tenants and owners may waive. When they do, you'll need to be aware of what's happening and how to handle it. The last thing you want is to follow an owner's illegal instructions. If you do, you can quickly find yourself in trouble as well. You are the professional. You are responsible for knowing what to do. During my time in the Army I was faced with plenty of people who were above me in rank. If you find yourself facing illegal orders, you must have the courage and the knowledge to handle the situation and know when to say no.
Owners aren't the only ones who might try to take advantage of a situation. We have all heard horror stories of bad tenants. You

will run into situations where people will lie on applications or during interviews. You will hear intricate stories about why the rent is late or why the window is broken. While it's impossible to have all perfect tenants all the time. You can have a majority of good tenants, and you can reduce the chances of things falling apart by taking a few upfront steps to make sure that you are only approving applications from the best possible applicants.

I can't tell you how many times I hear these "tenant horror stories" only to find out that if the owner or manager had taken a different approach to how they handled the leasing and application process in the first place, many of these "Horror Story" situations could have been avoided. I'll often meet with owners who try to self manage and they usually begin by telling me how bad the last tenant they had was, and how they don't want to do property management anymore because they are tired of "dealing with tenants."

Yet, usually within the first few minutes of speaking with these owners it's clear that if they had just followed some simple and effective guidelines with a procedure that was exactly the same for every single applicant, they could have saved lots of time, stress and money. We will discuss what these steps are in the chapter that discusses tenant screening.

Ultimately your role as a property manager will be varied. There are many moving parts when it comes to the management of properties, tenants and owners. If you are a real estate agent or broker you will most likely be managing properties on behalf of owners and investors. It will require some balancing acts on your part to manage all the moving parts. You will learn that the number one factor in successful property management is effective and proactive communication. If you can become good at keeping everyone in the loop and everything on schedule you will have good success as a property manager. You will find your accounts are all well taken care of if you are proactive and stay on top of tasks. All rents are being paid on time. Expenses are being monitored and controlled. Your maintenance schedules will be up to date, your work orders will be completed in a timely manner and you have communicated with all parties effectively and timely. This is what a successful property management business looks like.

A shabby management business is reactive rather than proactive. They don't find out there was a leak under the sink until the tenant moves out. They don't attempt to collect rent soon enough and too much time goes by without communication. In a poorly run management company there is a loss of control of maintenance and service calls resulting in higher costs for owners. There is also the extremely high cost of turnover and vacancy. If not handled properly it can take what would be a cash flowing property and turn it into a cash drain. If you are someone who has ever had to deal with a bad management company you know that they can quickly become the difference between making money and losing money.

Your number one duty as the manager is to work to achieve the objectives & goals of the property owners.

I'm pretty sure that no owner's goal is to have high vacancy and high expenses. In chapter 3 when we discuss meeting with owners and how to be prepared for earning their business, it's a good idea to find out what the owners objectives are, and tell him or her how you are going to help them achieve those goals and develop a plan that will help everyone execute on those objectives. This duty is first and foremost because it is the most important element of property management. It was the very element that was missing from the management company that I had hired a number of years ago. They had put their goals and objectives in front of mine and failed to uphold their duties. Without integrity it makes trust difficult. Integrity is simply defined as doing what's right, even when no one will know the difference. Always do what's right for your client.

Duty number two on the list of managers responsibilities, is to generate income for the owner. This means working to keep vacancy rates and expenses low and to make sure that rents are collected quickly and efficiently. Later chapters will discuss how to ensure maximum income is being generated from a property. When it comes to single family homes and condos this means setting the correct rental rate, screening and choosing the right tenants and managing expectations on both the tenant side, and the owner's side.

Choosing the right tenant is the single most impactful thing that you will do when it comes to property management. WIthout the right tenant, nothing good happens. I will go into further detail about the best ways to screen tenants and what questions to ask during the application process. But just know that almost everything will hinge on whether or not you have placed a quality tenant or not.

The third duty of the property manager is to; Preserve and/ increase the value of the investment property. If you do what's necessary to be proactive about your management tasks, this last responsibility will take care of itself automatically. By responding to and quickly taking care of maintenance issues; by communicating regularly with tenants and performing inspections during the lease period; and by being proactive about providing property reports to owners that provide details of how to most effectively preserve and maintain the property, you will certainly be successful in your property management duties.
Summary:
- Understand what property management is and what your role will be.
- Know your duties to your owners.
- Maintain professionalism deliver the best service possible to your owners.

CHAPTER 2 - MARKETING.

Using the latest digital and internet marketing techniques to promote yourself as a property manager.

* * *

This chapter is a crash course on how to promote your website through search engines and other online platforms. Let's be honest. Real estate is a competitive industry. Providing property management as one of your services can be a great way to differentiate yourself to property owners who are looking for alternatives to selling their home. More and more over the last few years, I have seen a dramatic jump in the number of homeowners who call our firm asking us to help them analyze whether or not to sell, or rent out their house.

The fact is that now, more than anytime in history, people are choosing to rent a home regardless of whether or not they can afford to buy. I have found that many of my tenant clients today are, strong income earners, have good credit, and low debt levels. They could certainly buy a house if they wanted to, but they *choose* to rent instead.

This growing "renter economy" provides a fantastic opportunity for real estate agents considering property management. On the one hand, where you have owners who would traditionally be sellers, they are now considering becoming landlords. This can provide a steady stream of houses and condos that will be available for management. When it comes to the buying side, you have what would normally be potential home-buyers, who are now choosing to become tenants. The rental business is booming and now is the time to get involved. But like any other business venture you will need to include some marketing strategies to generate business and get the word out about your management services.

In today's digital world, it can be easier (and harder) than ever to get your message out to the masses. Easy, because the tools for mass communication are available to almost anyone nowadays. But, because it is available to everyone - it can be harder than ever to rise above the noise and be noticed. So in a competitive industry like real estate and competitive marketing channels like Google and Facebook, it is more important now than ever to understand how to be effective in your marketing. I would also like to mention that a lot of the strategies and tactics that were working just 4 or 5 years ago, are now considered outdated and ineffective. The digital world moves fast. It is important that you keep abreast of the digital marketing industry as well. As many agents who are independent contractors know, we are responsible for promoting ourselves and landing our own clients. Having some current knowledge of how digital and internet marketing works in today's marketplace, will be key for you going forward.

I started learning about digital marketing back in 2006/2007. I was 26 years old and I had just started my own brokerage on a shoestring. I needed to learn how to generate some business, fast. As luck would have it, fate stepped in and introduced me not only to a few great friends, but also some great mentors. As I was working on building up my brokerage in late 2006, I met a gentleman who was prolific in fine homes renovations and development, an area of the business in which I had a lot of interest at the time. He had just taken on a new multi-million dollar renovation project and wanted to know if I could help him manage the project. I was very interested. I had a strong interest in learning about construction management at the time and this seemed like the perfect opportunity to learn. So we worked out a deal. I would use my spare time to manage his project, he would teach me what I wanted to know. Little did I know however, that during this time, not only would I learn about managing construction projects, but I would also be starting on a life-long path of learning about internet and digital marketing. It just so happened that the people involved in this project had a strong background in internet marketing and business, and had done very well in the industry. I was also lucky enough to become friends with some of these individuals and they were willing to share their knowledge with me too! How lucky could I be! Not only was I able to learn about construction, but now I was also on the path of becoming an expert in internet marketing. For the last 14 years I have learned and studied everything I could in internet marketing. Today I would consider myself an expert. These skills have served me well over the years and I am thrilled to share with you what I know.

When it comes to internet marketing, there is no shortage of information. Some of it good, most of it mediocre, and some that's downright dangerous to your online reputation. My hope in this book, is to help you understand a few key concepts and give you some strong fundamental practices you can put into use in your property management business on day one. These fundamental practices will be effective if done properly. There is so much information on internet marketing out there, we can't get into it all in one small book about property management. Unfortunately there is just way too much information on the subject. In the last 20 years the practice of digital and internet marketing has become extremely competitive, along with becoming more and more complex. From changing algorithms and search engine updates, to rapidly shifting consumer behavior and attention spans, digital marketing has become harder. I implore you to stay informed about search engine and digital marketing. Read and learn what you can about the solid principles, and best practices that the search engines recommend in their publications. This will prove to stand the test of time amidst the changing landscape of competition.

My goal is to provide two main things, Help you to know and understand the basics of how internet marketing works, and to provide you will a solid foundation of action steps that can be taken easily and have great results.

Know the Basics - Fundamentals of Search Engines and Digital Marketing.

Real estate and property management are very competitive when it comes to online marketing. You've probably heard it called by several names, digital marketing, internet advertising, SEO, PPC, web marketing, social marketing, etc. But as far as I'm concerned it's all the same thing. For the purposes of this book we will refer to it from now on as Digital Marketing or DM.

Digital marketing is the idea of using online resources to get a potential customers attention.

Most of us are familiar with two main types of Digital Marketing -

1. SEO or Search Engine Optimization. The practice of bringing traffic to your website from "organic search" traffic ....
2. PPC - Pay Per Click or simply, paid advertising.

What's important to remember is that PPC is paid advertising, and SEO is "free" (sort-of). Let's start by discussing what a search engine is and how it works in general. Then we can discuss the concepts of SEO and PPC and how to apply them to your business.

Wikipedia defines a search engine as, a computer program that searches for and identifies items in a database that correspond to keywords or characters specified by the user, used especially for finding particular sites on the World Wide Web.

We all understand the concept of finding information through search engines. Most of us have used Google or one of the big search engines to look for information at one point or another. If you're like me, you use it everyday. Using a search engine is simple. We type in some words, and look for results that match. Easy right? Well, it's easy for the user at least. That's the way it should be. We are living in an on demand world, and when we want to know something, we google it and find the answer. But what is going on behind the scenes? In the back-end of the search engine software, there is actually an estimated 2 billion lines of code. That's Billion with a B. So the question becomes, how did the question we asked Google, become the answer we received from Google?.... The answer lies in those 2 billion lines of code. The search engine itself is simply a computer program. Understanding how that computer program works will help you improve your digital marketing efforts. Below I will outline the benefits and disadvantages of both PPC and SEO.

When we use a search engine to find information, we enter keywords that we think should give us the correct result, then we scan the results page of all suggested websites, and hopefully find what we are looking for. Let's look at an example of what a SERP or Search Engine Results Page looks like and how to identify the difference between paid and organic SEO.

Search Engine Optimization: SEO - This is an online marketing strategy that involves bringing traffic to your website through organic traffic. Traditionally, SEO has been a very attractive strategy because technically it is free. You can get valuable traffic to your website at no additional cost. If you are able to earn a top spot in the organic search results, it can be a very beneficial to your online presence. Because of this low cost valuable traffic, everyone wants to get their website listed on the first page of the SERP's. But it's not really as easy as it sounds. Remember those 2 billion lines of code in Google's software? Those algorithms and lines of code are what is determining the websites you see in the results page. The game is how do we get our website to be one of those chosen results.

While it would be impossible to completely understand all the code that google uses, there are guideposts that Google provides, explaining how to best promote your website through their site. Google has created and is constantly updating, thousands of pages of documentation outlining what the best practices are. If you are inclined, you can read these guides at https://www.google.com/webmasters. There is a ton of free information here, and if you follow the rules you can get results for your website. But you must follow the guidelines. If you don't, your website will likely never be found among all the millions of possible results that google has to choose from.

How does a search engine choose which results to display? It's all done automatically through those billions of lines of code. But ultimately, the main purpose of a search engine is to provide relevant results to the user. They do this by weighing a bunch of data and various page ranking factors and determine what results are best based on the keywords entered by the user. The secret sauce for you will be to understand what those ranking factors are, and then figure out how to align your site and your content so that these factors are being addressed on your site. Google will reward you for this.

What are the page ranking factors that determine the search results? There are tons! But let's only focus on a few most important ones to start. The list below is not all encompassing but if you were to focus on only the 5 following factors, it would be very likely that you would get great results with your web marketing efforts.

But wait! Very important!** Before updating your page ranking factors you will want to take a deep dive on keyword research. It's very likely that the keywords you want to rank for, are not properly implemented on your site or in the site structure.

What is keyword research? Keyword research is the act of determining and predicting what words your customers will be using to find what they are looking for. There are a number of ways to conduct keyword research. There are paid and free tools that help analyze this information. The easiest place to start is with the google keyword tool. You will need an adwords account to use this tool but it is worth the effort. If you don't already have an Adwords account, please get one and start becoming familiar with how to use the software, especially the keyword research tool. There are other ways to conduct research as well. One of the best ways is to simply google the keywords you want to rank for, and analyze the results. This is also a great way to see who your competition is for these keywords. Remember to only look at the organic results when analyzing keywords and competition. Once you have a good keyword list of at least 15-20 solid keywords that you want to rank for, you will then begin updating your page ranking factors to increase your visibility to the search engines. *Note - Do not try to use more than one keyword phrase per webpage or blog post! Everyone makes this mistake. Trying to make your page encompass more than one keyword phrase will spread your keyword influence too thin, and you will end up not ranking for any of the search terms that you were attempting to be seen for.

What are the most important page ranking factors?
1. Page Structure.
2. Page Content
3. Links - Internal vs external
4. Location. Local search.
5. Social & Reviews

1. <u>Page Structure.</u> This part is a bit technical but so very important. If you have a website that you own, whether

you realize it or not, there is already something on your site called meta-data. Meta-Data is defined simply as "data about data." The metadata on your site tells the google software (robots) what your website is about. It is important that this information has an accurate description of what your website represents. Make sure that the description and keywords of your site in the page structure or meta-data are accurate and up to date. Most importantly this is referring to your title tags and your page description. Your webmaster or website provider should be able to help you with this. If this is something they won't do, find a better website provider. If they won't let you in your files or help you access and update them, something shady is going on and you might want to reconsider using a new host or website provider.

2. Page content. Page content is different than page structure and meta-data. Content is what your users and customers are going to see and read directly on your webpage. Meta-data is visible only to the search engines. Creating content should be your highest priority for your website. You may have heard the expression, "Content is King." This is an accurate expression. But it should be revised to say, Quality Content is King. So many people have been going through the motions of creating content, but mostly they are making a few posts on social media, and writing a blog post (once every 6 months). This is not quality content. There are also website providers that promote the service of creating and posting content for you. Do not be tricked by this. This will not help your search rankings. It is considered duplicate content. Duplicate content is potentially posted on hundreds of different websites in the exact same format. It is not unique to you and therefore the search engines will not reward you. You can check your articles to see whether or not they would be con-

sidered duplicate content by going to a free website called SIteliner at http://www.siteliner.com. Unfortunately there is no getting around doing the work of creating content. You will have to find some time to create content or hire someone to create it for you. But this can get very expensive. What kind of content should you create? Make it specific to your targeted keywords. Too many people create content just for the sake of putting something on a web page, or they don't have a solid list of highly targeted keywords that they focus on. But you want to be more strategic than that. Make sure you are creating content around your list of top keywords. Take one keyword or keyword phrase like "property management in Tampa, FL" and build a page full of content centered around just those words. Remember, be sure you are only targeting one keyword or keyword phrase per piece of content. Digital content can be anything from a blog post, a web page, a video or even an audio file or podcast. You will want to use these various types of content to promote your brand. Also consider the channel where this content will be viewed. Content that converts well on Google may not have the same effect on facebook, and vice versa. You will want to test different messages on different platforms and "channels" to see which work best for which. This can be tested and analyzed through paid advertising campaigns which we will discuss next, and also through the use of analytics. Which simply is software that keeps track of all the metrics on your website and generates a report that you can analyze. Google offers a free analytics product that I highly recommend installing to your website. In essence however, the most important thing you can do is create lots of quality content as often as you can.

3. <u>Links. Internal & external</u> - Links are an extremely important aspect of building your digital footprint and creating authority so that search engines will rank your

website at the top of your desired keywords. There are two main ways to focus on link building. Internal links and external links.

Internal Links - These are going to be links on your web pages and blog posts that link to other pages on your site. Building internal links is easy. It just requires that you create enough content to create a good internal linking structure. For example: let's say you are creating some content based around the local keywords "property management in Tampa." You write at least 500 words on the topic, and within those 500 words about property management, maybe you mention the process of screening a tenant. It will behoove you then create some content about the topic of screening a tenant and link to it from your property management article by hyperlinking the phrase screening a tenant. You will also find a way to link back to your property management content from your tenant screening content as well.. And round and round it goes. Linking articles and posts to each other throughout your site is the essence of internal link building.

External Links - External links can be more challenging. Essentially, these are links from other sites and resources that link directly to your site. Google holds external links in high regard. They have been considered for a long time to be the most important factor to getting good SEO and high rankings in the results pages. In the early days of search marketing, entire services and businesses sprung up in response to the importance of external link building. However, please beware that many of these services are not acceptable in the eyes of google. 99% of them are going to be putting your entire website at risk of being penalized, or possibly even delisted from Google all together. If you are found to be participating in link building schemes it can destroy your web marketing efforts overnight. Google's engineers are smarter than we are. If you do it you will probably be caught. Stay away from services that claim they can get you external links fast. They can't. Not legitimately anyway. There are plenty of link building techniques however that are legitimate, and once you do start earning external links you will see you search engine rankings grow considerably. Some link building strategies are to simply ask another website to link to you... Of course you will have to deal with high rejection rates but if you are able to get someone to say yes, then you have struck gold. The only caveat to this is try and make sure the site that is linking to you has some relevance or relatedness to your site or service regarding content and context. Guest blog post, news articles, local neighborhood associations... Etc... Also please note that posting on facebook or other social media has very little SEO value. Google will not recognize links from sites like FB, instagram or other big "social media" sites and giant directories. The key will be to network with related services in your field and get them to link to you. If you can find the time to write, find online publications that will publish your articles and also provide you with links. This is not an overnight exercise. It will take time. But if you make an effort in your link building, you will see results.

4. <u>Location. Local search.</u> - Local search is one of the fastest growing, and in my opinion, most important strategies for not only local businesses but for large corporations as well. For a long time it was believed that local search was only for small businesses with one location. But that's no longer the case. Everything is somewhere. Many brokerages and offices have multiple locations, and if you don't have a strategy to address local SEO you are missing the boat. When it comes to local search, it's not just about the physical location of your office or business. One of the fastest growing keyword searches is "___ near me." For property managers and real estate agents, that could read, "homes for rent near me"

or "property managers near me," and if you know how to leverage the key components of what search engines look for in a local search, you are in a better position to show up in the top of the results. So what is it that Google and the other search engines look for when it comes to local search? First, is the geo-modifier with geo- standing for geographic. This is a simple as putting the name of the city or town in front of the key word. If you are publishing content about property management, add a geo-modifier like Tampa property management. Simple right? However, adding a geo-modifier is only one step in the process. Right now, Google is the biggest influencer in the local search market. They have recently taken a number of steps to grow their local influence. This is a great opportunity for all local search marketing. Google is currently promoting a free service called "google my business." This is going to have a lot of influence on your local presence regarding search engines. It has a lot of great features and you will want to make sure that you use as many of these features as possible. I'm not going to go into every feature of the Google My Business listing but it holds a lot of influence over your local presence so be sure to create your local business page and try not to leave anything blank. If it asks you to upload some pictures of your business, make sure you do. Ensure all fields are complete and accurate. You will be rewarded for this if you do it right. This will also be where you should direct your customers when asking for reviews. Reviews and ratings are very important as well, and we will get into them on the next section.

5. Social & Reviews - I have lumped social media marketing and reviews into the same category because I feel as though they go hand in hand. Let's define social media marketing. When I refer to social media, this includes, facebook, instagram, linkedin, snapchat, or any other

"social" platform that you may be aware of or partici-pate in. There are also many services and businesses out there today that are offering to give you an edge when it comes to social media marketing. Personally I wouldn't hire any of these companies. They may provide some value depending on what your business objectives are, but for the most part, there isn't anything they will do for you that you can't do for yourself. (Note: I'm not re-ferring to paid ads on these platforms, we will discuss paid advertising in the next section). The social media marketing I am referring to in this section are the or-ganic aspects of the platform. The essence of social media is communication. Yet I see so many people who just post something about their service that is about them only. It's a typical "look at me" post that offers practically nothing to your audience and simply be-comes filler for your social efforts. The real key to social media marketing will be communicating directly to those you are trying to reach. Figure out how to provide value and connect with those who are looking for the value or the solutions you can provide. This will require you to also go "off page" which means finding other pages and people who you want to connect with and start communicating with them directly. It seems sim-ple to say but so many people simply automate their posting to post random stuff in hopes that people will engage with it. Or they just post things like, "looking to sell your house? Call me!" I would be willing to bet that only works 1 out of 100 times. Really effective social media marketing requires old fashioned one-on-one communication. Search out those who you would like to connect with, and message them or make comments on their posts. But not just any comments. Be specific and provide a solution to their problem. In fact, do not promote your service at all. Simply give something of value and expect nothing in return. This is really the only true effective social media marketing. When it comes to making posts that you are hoping will engage with large amounts of people, leave that to paid advertising. Granted, you want to post links and articles that lead back to your website. But when it comes to organic social media, slow down. Put in the work and give something for nothing. Make it about them and you will see your true, genuine connections grow. Same thing goes for reviews.

When it comes to reviews, people don't really want to take the time to sit down and write a review. The most motivated review writers tend to be people who are angry or upset at you and no matter what, there will always be those individuals. Don't focus on them. Just focus on providing good service and the good reviews will come. But you have to ask for them. That's why developing real connections with your customers is so important. Be persistent and polite. You may have to ask a few times before people actually do the review so just keep reminding them. When you do get reviews, be sure to follow two main rules. Rule number 1; respond. You should always respond to your reviews. Clearly if it's a positive review the response is easy. A simple thank you or whatever the situation calls for will suffice. But if it's a negative review, follow rule number two before you respond. Rule 2 is: Be professional. No matter what the negative review says, no matter how wrong or incorrect the person is, you must respond professionally. Do not get into an argument or try to defend your position. Your ego will want to. But don't do it! Here's why. You're not actually responding to the person who wrote the review. Technically it may seem that you are, but you're not. Your response is actually there for other potential customers who might read it. Most people will dismiss a few negative reviews when it comes to choosing a service provider. Especially if the business responds professionally and with empathy and concern to the person who wrote the negative review. So don't worry about them. Write a response that you want other potential customers to read and think that even though you had a customer who was unsatisfied, you're clearly making an effort to improve and provide better service in the future. That's the perception you want to create.

If you focus on those 5 main categories when developing your web presence you will see results. The world of search marketing and SEO is vast. You will never learn it all. There is too much to cover and some if it is just too technical to even bother with.

However, another important factor that isn't in the list above but is definitely worth mentioning is what's called, page load speed. You can check your page speed for free through the google developer tools at https://developers.google.com/speed/pagespeed/insights/ - the report that is genenrated will give you a wealth of information regarding the loading speed of your website. Google has said directly that page load speed is an important factor when it comes to SEO. It is believed that page speed does affect your ranking. The information you will get from the PageSpeed Insights report will be a bit technical. If you have a webmaster who handles the technical side of your site, give them this report and ask them to make the suggested changes. If you are interested in learning how to do it yourself, then feel free to dive in and get acquainted with the aspects on your website that affecting the loading speed.

Some common questions that people ask are:
- How long does it take to get SEO results?

The answer is it depends. Don't expect much for about 60 days. But the truth is count on 6 months or so. Not to mention that SEO is always evolving and is a constant practice. The best thing to do is get in a habit of consistently writing and creating content. Stick with it and follow the rules, and eventually you'll get some traction.

- How can I ensure that only certain pages are displayed on the SERP?

You can't. The search engines decide what pages they want to display. If you focus on your specific keywords and follow the rules you can have a likely result, but there is no guarantee when it comes to organic SEO. This is one of the main differences between paid advertising and SEO. With paid ads you have full control over what pages and content are promoted. With SEO it's up to the search engines. Which leads us into the next section - Paid Ads.

Paid Advertising -
Paid Ads or PPC which stands for Pay Per Click. Is a form of advertising on search engines that allows the advertiser to have full control on what's displayed and what's seen. The results are also immediate and on demand. Just like going to the grocery store when you need food, you can buy search ads when you need traffic to your website. Paid advertising is unique and has many different characteristics from SEO. The strategies are also much different and it will be important for you to understand these differences so that you can be successful in your paid advertising efforts.

As you read this, many of you might be saying, "I tried pay per click, it didn't work. It was expensive and I didn't get any results." That is completely understandable. If you don't know what you're doing, you can blow through your budget in two seconds with no results. Of course you would think it doesn't work! However, I have to be honest here - it's your fault it didn't work. Google and Bing and Facebook make billions of dollars on advertising revenue. If it didn't work, no one would do it. But you have to be sure you're doing it right. Most people don't. This section will hopefully help you figure out why it didn't work and to correct the issues you had so you can move forward with more success.

It's been said that when it comes to search marketing, paid advertising is equal parts science and art. Without the right creative displays, headlines, or calls to action it won't work. But if you don't understand how to read the data and implement that information effectively, your beautiful and creative designs will never be seen by the right people.

Start with your keywords. Choosing the right keywords in your paid ad campaigns will be the first major step. As a real estate agent, have you ever run a paid ad campaign with the keywords "Real Estate" - Everytime I ask that question I inevitably get people who say, yes of course! I cringe every time.

Here's why. Do me a favor, put this book down and do a web search using the keywords "real estate". What are the top results? As of this writing, the top results are; Zillow.com, Trulia.com and Realtor.com... These are the largest and most successful real estate websites in the world. Are you telling me you want to compete with these companies? Don't even try! These businesses have huge budgets and huge influence. You have no chance. As an individual agent you have to be creative. Use keywords that include geo-modifiers. Use keywords that identify your niche. Use longer keyword strings for a more targeted effect such as "real estate agents near me in Tampa, FL" or maybe instead of just "property management" try "property managers for condos" be specific. Yes there will be less traffic for these types of keywords, but your budget will stay under control and the traffic you do get will be much higher quality since the keywords are more specific. Which is the name of the game, quality over quantity. Let's get into how to maximize quality in your paid ads.

Match type. Did you know that there is a difference between the keywords property manager the keywords "property manager" and the keywords [property manager]? Do you know what the differences are? Yes, one has quotes and another has brackets but in the world of search engines there is a major difference. The difference is what is called match type. These are settings in the google ad platform that that allow you to make some specific requirements to how and when your ads are displayed. Many people are not aware of this and it is the number one reason why people see their ad budget get blown out of the water without any results. Let's say you decide to run some paid ads on the google platform. During the process google will have you add the keywords you want your advertisements to be displayed for. You add your keywords and move on to the next step. But what you don't realize is that you have just set your keywords to a "broad match" match type. This is the default setting for Google, but it is the most ineffective keyword setting there is. There are three types of match types. Broad Match, Phrase Match and Exact Match. Each one has very distinct characteristics. For example, if you are planning to use the keywords real estate agent and you have it set to a broad match, what you may not realize is that your ads can show up under almost any combination of those words, with the most likely scenario being that you will show up for the search "real estate" without the word "agent." Even though you thought you were just getting traffic for the entire keyword string, because it was set as a broad match, you still showed up under the term real estate. Do you remember the problem we discussed previously about that very general phrase? It's not specific enough and even though you thought you were being specific, because it was a broad match google showed your ad even when someone just typed the words real estate. In turn this will show your ads to the wrong people, your budget will be maxed out, and you will get very poor results. The solution to this is to make sure that when you are creating your ad campaigns, your keyword settings are set to either phrase match or exact match. Phrase match says to google that you only want your ads shown to people who include all the words of your keyword string. So if your keyword string is real estate agent, then phrase match will ensure that your ads will be shown only to people who have all those words in their query. The big difference between phrase match and exact match is that phrase match could have additional words such as real estate agent for buying a home or a different order to the words, etc. While exact match requires the exact words in the exact order. I tend to recommend phrase match simply because unless your keyword is getting huge traffic exact match will exclude too many people. There is definitely a time and a place to use exact match but just be aware that this will create your smallest audience. So when setting up your advertising campaign be sure to check your keyword settings and use at least a phrase match. This will help you keep your budget in check and you will have higher quality conversions which is what's really important.

Landing pages. If you have run paid ads before, where did you send the visitors who clicked on the ad? Did you send them to your homepage? I hope not! But it's likely that you did. This is a huge mistake that I see people making. DO NOT use your homepage in a paid campaign, ever. Remember those blog posts and keyword specific pages you've been writing, send them there. If you wrote a post about property managers for single family homes, your ad needs to have a set of keywords that would match up with that intent, and then make sure your ad links directly to that page discussing property managers of single family homes. Take them right to the related content, or landing page. It's called a landing page because they will land on it directly from the ad. Don't leave it up to your customer to find the info from home home page, they will simply just leave. This will have a huge impact on your conversion rates and Google will reward you for this as well. Always use landing pages and never send people to your homepage within a paid ad campaign.

I could write an entire book dedicated to the ideas and strategies of digital marketing. Not to mention is is a constantly evolving industry that needs to be kept up with. The scope of the subject is too vast to be covered in this short book. But check my blog for more updated info and other strategies that I write about at https://PropertyManagementPete.com

Summary:
- Learn all you can about how digital marketing works
- Understand what keywords are best for you
- Focus on creating quality content
- Utilize the strategies for both paid and organic marketing
- Continue to learn

CHAPTER 3 - MEETING WITH PROPERTY OWNERS AND INVESTORS

* * *

Now that you have maximized your digital marketing efforts and you have a steady stream of new leads from which you will book appointments, you will want to get prepared for your meetings so that you can close the deal and get started managing properties. Meeting with property owners and investors is different from your typical listing appointment. It's a very different type of transaction and they will want to hear certain things from you regarding your services. In this chapter we will cover the possible various needs your client might have and how to inform they regarding how you will be of service. There may also be a slight difference between a homeowner who wants to rent out a house they own or lived in, vs. a professional investor who owns properties for the sole purpose of renting them out for income. I will break these individuals into two categories and address each one. They may have different goals and ideas about what it means to have a property management company handling their property. Identify which category your client falls into, and be sure you are offering the correct support to their situation. Obviously there will be many similarities in the service and the basic principles of property management will always apply. The differences however, will most likely be in terms of mindset, and how you communicate certain ideas will be the biggest difference. For example if your client is a homeowner turned landlord, this could be the first time they have ever dealt with renting out real estate, and they may also have certain attachments to the home that an investor owner would not. Knowing what words and language to use will be key. Most importantly, is to ask questions and listen to the needs of your client. Understanding their goals and providing solutions is the recipe for success in any business relationship.

Property Owners/Homeowners -

More and more we are meeting with people who are first time landlords, often called "accidental landlords." This is a term for people who may have a home that they purchased years ago and then lost their equity in the real estate crash of 2009 or through some other financial hardship. They find themselves in a situation where they can't sell the house, so they decide to rent it out instead. Other times we see individuals who purchased a home, but are forced to relocate due to family, or a job or even military service. They may not want to sell the home because they plan on moving back to the area later or they got a good deal on the house and feel that renting it out will allow them to cover the payments without coming out of pocket, and possibly even net a few extra dollars every month, without actually having to sell it. If you know what kind of situation your client is facing it will help you to better serve their needs. All clients want to know that you will preserve their property and in fact it is your duty as a property manager to do so. But when it comes to a homeowner who is renting out their house for the first time they may have some special requests that a typical investor won't. Pay attention to what their concerns are and be sure to address them during your meeting. The most important thing is to set clear expectations so that your owner understands exactly how the process works as this will likely be the first time they have used a property management company. For example, I remember an owner calling us one time and wanting to know why the rent was late. It was the 2nd day of the month and the tenant had actually paid a couple of days early, so I was confused at why the owner thought the rent was late. But what they meant was, why wasn't the rent in their account by the second day of the month.... But had the agreement been more carefully reviewed with the owner they would have known that owners are generally paid out around the 10th of the month. But they thought that rent should have been immediately sent into their account. They were a first time rental owner and they were not clear on how the process worked. What I didn't know, and came to realize, was that they had their mortgage payment due on the first. They had recently been relocated by their employer, and between rent on the new place and the mortgage on the house they owned, the money was short every month without the rent income. I had not been aware of this until now. But it did present a potential problem. While I was able to arrange to have the rent payments rushed processed every month to help reduce the lag time between payments, there was nothing I would be able to do about unexpected repairs and maintenance. When it comes to owning rental properties, repairs and maintenance are an eventual certainty and if the owner doesn't have any reserves to take care of these problems things can quickly go downhill. Especially if the repairs are something that is required by law. If they are left undone, the owner and you as the property manager can be held liable. So, the lesson here is make sure your owners are one hundred percent clear on what having a rental property will be like. Try to cover possible scenarios and prepare them for how the process will work and what is required of them as landlords. A few things that you will want to remember is, like we covered in the above example, know what their situation is and why they are deciding to rent out their home. Have a clear breakdown of what the costs will be to a homeowner not just for your service fees, but have estimates of what certain things could cost when they need repair or replacement. Do a good walk-through with the owner and point out anything that you think may need addressing sooner than later. Expectations will be everything for new owners and accidental landlords, do your best to set them up for success.

Investor Clients -

When it comes to owners and clients who are more experienced in dealing with rental property they may be wanting to hear certain things as well. These things will likely be based on prior experiences they may have had in dealing with tenants or other property managers. Be sure to ask them what they expect from the relationship.

Investors are generally here to make money. They weren't forced into the situation based on circumstances. They have certain financial goals and metrics in mind. Find out what they are and determine if you can add value. Most recently I had a property owner who had always handled the property himself and wanted to know how we could add value. After discussing it we determined that it was taking him about twice as long to get a unit ready for rent than it would have taken us. Even though he was going to pay a little more to have the work done by us, we were going to save him thousands of dollars in the course of the year just by being able to get his units leased faster and reduce his vacancy rate.

Another case that comes to mind is an owner who had mortgage payments on his property. Or as investors refer to it, debt service. He told me that based on the cost of his debt service he couldn't afford to pay a full service management company and was looking for a discount option. After some digging around we found out that his units were underpriced based on the market. We were able to show him that by making some small improvements and increasing the rents he could make more money than he thought possible. This was going to improve his ROI (return on Investment) in the long run and more than cover our fees.

When it comes to homeowners and accidental landlords they will want to feel comfortable that you will be taking care of their home and helping them through the process. When it comes to investors they tend to be more numbers driven and want to know that you are keeping a close eye on the bottom line.

No matter what kind of owner you are serving, the number one most important factor that will set you apart from other managers is communication. Owners want to know that you are going to be keeping them informed with all matters. No one likes surprises, especially when you are in charge of handling someone's most important asset(s). Communicating and being accountable will be factors that will make or break you a property manager.

Understanding what the goals of your owners are, understanding their challenges and communicating with them on all matters will ensure you are providing the best service possible.

Summary:
- Understand who your client is and what their mindset will be.
- Know the owner's situation and be sure that expectations are clear.
- Let them know how you will add value to their situation.
- Communicate with your owners at all times

CHAPTER 4 - HOW TO PRICE AND PREPARE RENTAL UNITS FOR MAXIMUM PROFIT.

* * *

Determining the rental price of your unit is a key factor to attracting the right tenants, and having it ready for showings will ensure that your unit leases quickly and for the highest rate possible.

Like in a sales transaction, correct pricing can make or break your listing. When it comes to rentals even the smallest adjustment can make a big difference. I have seen rental listings that would sit vacant with very little showing activity, and sometimes all it took was a $50 or even $25 dollar price reduction in the monthly rent amount to move the needle and start getting interested applicants. The monthly rental price in the leasing market can be very sensitive. It will be your job to help the owner discover the best price for their unit.

As a real estate agent you are probably familiar with providing home sellers (and buyers) with price analysis reports often times called a CMA. Most times this is done before a listing agreement to help a home seller understand how to effectively price their home for sale. A rental listing is very similar, except instead of using data on homes that have recently sold, you are using rental data from homes that have recently been leased. Unfortunately, finding this information is not always as easy as when you look up sales data. It is more common for there to be a larger database of sales prices than there are rental prices. Many times a lease transaction is not done through the MLS system and seldom are they recorded in public records, so it might take a little more digging on your part to determine the best price. But do not fear, because nowadays there are more and more software solutions that can help you with your rental pricing strategy. One of my favorite tools is a website called RentOmeter.com. This is a freemium type of web based software that is very helpful when it comes to pricing your rentals. They focus specifically on aggregating rental data based on recency and location to determine an accurate range of potential pricing. Clearly, like any home, whether it's for sale or for rent, the condition and the location will play a major factor into your analysis, and when it comes to rentals, there can be drastic differences from one house or apartment to another, even if they are in the same neighborhood and sometimes even the same building. Tenants will often have different priorities than homebuyers. The outlook on their budget is different and their needs may differ as well. When pricing your units, visit the property and inspect the unit. See what the amenities are and what the condition the unit is in. One tenant may not care that the kitchen is dated as long as there is in-unit laundry, where another tenant needs to have granite countertops and stainless steel appliances, even if they have to walk 3 flights of stairs to get to a shared laundry room.

The main factors that will influence a rental unit tend to be, updates and condition of the unit itself. Laundry facilities (in-unit or shared), parking, and pet policies. Of course there are plenty of other factors that may go into the tenants consideration, but through my experience, these tend to be some of the top factors.

Let's discuss the influence of pet policies when it comes to leasing. Ultimately it will be up to the owner to decide if they want to accept pets. However, when possible I always attempt to get owners to accept pets. Here's why; many people have pets. A large majority of renters have a dog or cat. So when you allow pets you are opening yourself up to a much larger pool of potential applicants, which is always good. Research has also shown that when people are allowed to bring their pets, they are more willing to settle in for a longer duration tenancy. They feel more at home and are more likely to to stay. Whenever you can reduce turnover it will save your owner money, and they will certainly appreciate that. The potential drawbacks could be things like pet odors and potential damage to the house or unit. However, this can be mitigated with pet rent and/or pet deposits. You would be surprised how many people are willing to spend an extra $40 a month on rent just so they can have their cat or dog living with them. We always recommend allowing pets. But you will want to have the owner "pet-proof" the house as much as they can. If possible make sure they have tile or hard surface floors that can be easily cleaned. If they do have carpets, you will want to make the sure the tenant is responsible for paying for a professional carpet cleaning upon vacating. Also make sure you have a provision against what are considered "dangerous breeds." There tends to be a lot of controversy over what is considered a dangerous breed. For the purposes of this discussion, a dangerous breed is whatever the insurance company says it is. Because that's the real purpose of the clause. If there were to be an incident, the owner could have a claim on their property insurance. Be sure that you help the owner remain in compliance with their policy. Always seek a legal professional in these matters as well. It will be worth it in the end.

Updating the unit. I remember walking through a property one time with an owner after a previous tenant had bailed on him and we were discussing the plan for finding him a good tenant quickly.

As I walked the unit with him I would point out certain things and mention that we should make some updates. I noticed the carpet was quite stained and I mentioned that some new flooring would go a long way. "No, I don't want to pay for that he said." Ok I thought, not the end of the world, a heavy duty steam cleaning might do the trick... Then I said; "We should definitely paint the unit - it will really brighten the place up and eliminate some of these wear marks on the walls and doors." "No" he said again, "the walls are fine..." 0 for 2 at this point. Lastly, I opened the refrigerator to find it stained, dirty and smelling awful, well beyond being able to be cleaned. Don't worry I told him we have a great connection for refurbished appliances at a very good cost. Again, all he said was, "No, I'll just have it cleaned." It was at that moment that I realized we would not be able to manage this man's property. I now understood why he was getting trouble tenants and having a hard time renting his units.

Like a home buyer, a renter will want to have the best upgrades possible in their rental unit. They don't have to be super high end. But everyone should have a nice clean place. Also, just like in the selling of a property, the best upgrades and updates to make tend to exist in specific areas. These areas are, kitchens, bathrooms, flooring and paint. However, when it comes to leasing, tenants tend to be willing to overlook certain things that someone who's purchasing the home might not. But, it will always be a good idea to ensure the unit is clean, odor free and freshly painted. Depending on the price point of the rental it may not be necessary to have the granite counters or the highest end appliances, but it will be important to offer a clean and freshly painted rental. If the owner is not willing to invest in these basic necessities then that could be a red flag for you as a manager. The last thing you want is to work for an owner who is unwilling to do what's necessary to ensure the unit is in good shape. Run far and fast from these types of owners.

Another topic that may come up is whether to have the unit furnished or not. Many owners may have been living there and want to know if it's a good idea to keep it furnished. It depends on a number of factors. If it's a short term rental, then yes, it's probably a good idea to have the unit furnished. It's just easier that way if people will only be there a few months or less. However when it comes to longer term leases, such as 7 or more months at a time, I always recommend to the owner not to furnish the unit. For pictures and showings there can be some benefit to having a home that's furnished or staged even if possible. We have had rentals staged before, but these were for very high end properties. But what we have found though is that most of the time, for a long term rental, it is best to provide an unfurnished unit. It has been shown that when people are bringing their own belongings and their own furniture, they tend to feel more committed and will stay longer and take better care of the property. It's probably due to the fact that if people are taking the time to bring their stuff and make purchases and invest in the tenancy, then they are more likely to feel at home and stay longer and be overall better tenants.

Summary:
- Use available software like your local MLS, and rentometer to help determine accurate pricing.
- Encourage owners to accept pets and prepare for them.
- Make updates to the most important areas of the unit, such as kitchens, bathrooms, flooring and paint.
- Don't work with owners who aren't willing to invest in their property.

CHAPTER 5 - HOW TO EFFECTIVELY ADVERTISE YOUR RENTAL UNITS

* * *

Now you're ready to start marketing your units to the public. This is one of the most important steps in making sure your that not only is your unit leased to the best possible tenant, but also to make sure that you use the marketing tools and listing information to help you eliminate time wasting showings with tenants who may not qualify or may not be interested in your unit due to certain features.

It can be natural to want to get as many showings as possible. The activity will look good to the owner and you want as many people as you can get exposed to the unit. But when it comes to leasing you can definitely waste a lot of time on the wrong people. We will discuss this further when it comes to screening tenants but some of the rules apply in this chapter as well.

Like a sales listing, put your best foot forward right off the bat. The time in which you will have the most interest in the listing is within the first couple of weeks. Have as much info about the property as you can and write a good description. Discuss some of those important factors from chapter 4 such as fresh paint, new flooring, laundry, pets and parking too if applicable. You don't want to not mention the laundry situation just to find out when you meet the tenant for a showing that they need to have in-unit laundry and it's a deal breaker without it. So have a well written description that highlights those desirable features along with any other amenities that may be desirable.

Within the listing description you will also want to outline the general terms of the lease and any applicable fees. If the unit is only available for long term lease like 12 or more months, you don't want to be doing a showing just to find out the tenant wants a short term lease. So make it clear. Also disclose any fees that may apply such as application or HOA fees. You'll also want to outline the income and credit requirements. This will help the tenant to understand if they can afford the unit and it will also let prospective applicants that there will be a thorough application process and this will help to eliminate some of the riff-raff that may otherwise try to pull a fast one on you. We will go into greater detail on this when it comes to tenant screening, but just by mentioning that you have strict guidelines in place will help.

Pictures. Take lots of pictures. It's been proven that listings with lots of good photos will always get more interest from tenants and prospects. Most of us have a smartphone that will take quality photos. Be sure to take plenty of pictures of all the main areas and also of the common areas as well. The last thing you want is to get home and find out you don't have any good pictures for your listing or that you forgot to snap some photos of important areas. Follow some basic guidelines when taking pictures. Use the "landscape" format when shooting. Many websites and MLS's require the images to be shot in landscape. If they aren't, they won't look right on the listing. Also, do your best to have the unit cleaned up and looking orderly. If the apartment or house is occupied it may be more difficult, but try and give the owner or the tenant some heads up as to when you will be taking pictures so that it can be cleaned up and organized as best as possible. Turn on lights and get many different angles of the same room. You will often find that the picture you thought looked good, turned out to be not so great when you got home.

Websites - there are lots of great websites available for advertising your rental listing, and it is my personal opinion that craigslist is not one of them. There was a time when craigslist was the best, but that has waned. This certainly depends on your market of course, but for the agents in our office, we find it's more trouble than it's worth. The last several listings we put on craigslist generated nothing but robocalls from services we didn't want or outright scammers. If you do use craigslist, I recommend watermarking your pictures. We have found that the best way to market our rental listings on the largest number of websites is right through our MLS. Yes you will have to pay a leasing fee to an agent but it's worth it, especially if it helps you get your unit rented faster. The MLS in our market here in the Tampa Bay area uses what's called, listing syndication, which will disseminate your listing to dozens of other real estate portals and websites out there. I have found that many MLS's around the country do the same. This will save you tons of time in your marketing efforts. The places where your listing is, the more potential tenants who will be able to find it. Our MLS also automatically watermarks the images to help protect you from intellectual property theft (other agents and services using your images), and scammers who will try to close your listing and divert the leads to themselves in hopes of manipulating someone out of a security deposit and rent. It is a very real threat going on in the marketplace right now and I have seen it personally way more times than I'd like. So I feel that the safest and most effective way to market your listings is on the MLS. Now if you're not a member of an MLS or don't have access, then as of this writing, the real estate website Zillow seems to be the most effective for marketing rentals. Say what you want about Zillow but they are they have a large syndication network themselves and have recently put a lot of development into providing tools for leasing agents and landlords.

Another source of marketing for your listings can be your previous tenants and tenants who are looking to move around that time frame who may be a match for the property. These are great leads because you already know who they are. You are aware of their behavior and payment history and whether or not they would be a good fit. I can't tell you how many times we will have tenants whose lease is expiring around that same time and are looking to move. We are able to simply move them from one unit right into another! It's fantastic. Of course if you're newer to the leasing game, you may not have an extensive list of tenants to choose from. Find out from other agents in your office if they know of anyone looking to lease a house or apartment. You can also look on the MLS for agents who leased a similar property about a year ago and approach them directly to see if their tenant is looking to move.

Lastly I'll recommend this. Once your listings are up and running, answer your phone! The leasing business moves fast. Tenants will just move on and call someone else if you're not there to field the call. Make sure you answer the phone and you will have that much more success just from that one thing!

Summary:
- Have a complete and accurate description of the property and leasing process.
- Use lots of pictures and format them correctly.
- List on your MLS or other major real estate websites.
- Connect with previous tenants and other leasing agents.
- Answer your phone!

CHAPTER 6 - SHOWING AND SCREENING APPLICANTS.

* * *

This is probably one of the most important steps in the whole process. You will be meeting with people you don't know, to show them a home that they may be moving into. Unlike a home sale where you may never speak to the buyer again, when you are managing a rental property, you will often times have frequent contact with the resident. You will want a thorough and effective screening system in place. There are also a number of fair housing laws that you will need to adhere to no matter what. I want to say also that I am not a lawyer or an expert on fair housing laws. There are certain guidelines that are in our company policies and they are never to be violated. I will share some of those guidelines here with you in this chapter. Always follow the fair housing laws and the instructions of your broker.

Recently I had an owner of a rental property tell me that he didn't want to manage his rental anymore and that he was getting out of the business. He goes on to tell me a story about how he had this terrible tenant that wrecked the house and didn't pay. I asked him how he found this tenant and he said that the person had lived in the neighborhood and had called when he saw this house go up for rent. The owner did no background checks or application and was surprised that the tenant didn't work out! After this bad tenant had finally moved out, the owner set about doing repair work on his rental house. While he was working on it a neighbor came over and asked if it was for rent. Sure was the owner said! The person said they were looking to move soon and would like to rent the house. Once again, this owner let the person move in with no background check or income verification. Needless to say, less than 6 months later he was having to evict the tenant and was facing another wrecked apartment. If he had just followed a simple tenant screening process he could have avoided all the drama and cost of those destructive residents.

When showing a unit to a prospective tenant there is always one main question that I always ask. The question is designed to provide me with insight as to what kind of tenant they may be. The answer will often raise a "red flag." While these responses are never exactly the same for everyone, nor do they guarantee that it will result in an application denial, it is a great starting point to help you in the screening process.

Often times the question can be asked and answered during the very first phone conversation and help you determine the next set of questions or to whether or not you even want to set up a showing. During the first contact with a possible applicant I always ask one main question, and that question is; "When are you looking to move?" While it may seem like a very normal question, and it is - there is a certain response that I am looking for. Nine times out of ten, if the response is, "As soon as possible!" Raise a red flag. While it's true that some people may have a legitimate reason for needing to move quickly, it's my experience that someone who is in a tremendous rush is running from another tenancy situation and they want to lock in their next place before the eviction hits. It's the most valuable question I ask, and it has saved me tons of headaches. There are lots of owners who think that it's a great response because their thinking that they will be able to rent their unit sooner than later and avoid vacancy costs. Don't be tempted by this. Most of the time it ends up badly. Now, of course, like I said, there can be legitimate reasons why someone needs to move-in quickly, so you don't want to just end the process if they say those magic words. But if they do seem to be in a rush the next question I ask is plain and simple. I'll say; "Why do you need to move so quickly?"At this point listen closely. If they start telling you about how the last landlord didn't fix a thing, and the place is a wreck and they need to get out of there as soon as possible, etc, etc, this is a problem tenant. I would almost guarantee it. Now we have two red flags. At this point I usually give them the rundown of what the requirements are, the amount of the application fee, the required proof of income, the credit and background check, and the rental history check. Ninety nine percent of the time I never hear from them again. They know at this point that we are professional operation and that all the boxes will need to be checked in order for them to be approved and they know that will never happen, so they move on. The fact is that most responsible people are aware of their upcoming move and take plenty of time to line up the next home or apartment. Of course there are certainly times in which someone has a real reason for a quick move. These folks will usually tell you things like, they just got a new job and they are from out of town and are on a time crunch, or the house they were living in had been sold and they weren't aware of the sale until the last minute and sometimes they may have had a place lined up but, through no fault of their own, it fell through with only a week or two left to move. These things can and do happen. Just give everyone the same spiel. Everyone. All the time. If you use the same words and the same process for every person you meet with you can never be accused of discrimination. Treat everyone exactly the same and just move them through the process in the same way, always.

Ok, now it's time for setting up showings. I like to generally go about showings in two ways, and which way I go will depend on a few factors. If you're in a hot market and the rental is well priced, you will be getting a LOT of calls. In this scenario it will be in your best interest to set up showings in a shot-gun style schedule. Set up showing times that are on the same one or two days only 15-20 minutes apart for each prospect. One thing you will learn when dealing with rentals is that people are much more likely to stand you up than in a home purchase situation. So this helps you eliminate a ton of back and forth for no-shows. It also creates a competitive situation. If the unit appears to be popular and busy with showings, there will be a greater sense of urgency among the applicants. Now, if the market is slower or the unit is a higher priced property you may not have the same level of activity. In this case simply set up showings as you would similar to when you are showing a home that's for sale. Just be sure to ask the qualifying questions and make sure you confirm the showing a short time beforehand.

Ok ,so you had some showings and there is some interest. When it comes time to have your prospects fill out an application, you will want to charge them a fee. Again, charge the same fee all the time, but you must charge a fee. Just by having an application fee you will eliminate a lot of the tire kickers and unqualified individuals. They know for the most part whether or not they will qualify and they don't want to waste $50 or $60 bucks to find out what they already knew. So you must charge a fee. Not to mention you will be running a credit and background check and those aren't free, so you'll want to cover your costs as well. Make sure your application asks for all the pertinent data. Drivers license number, social security number, current and previous address, etc. You can check out my blog at propertymanagementpete.com for a sample application. Many of the popular software solutions have an online application and using this feature will be the most effective way to go. If you do use paper applications, be sure to keep copies at your office in a secure file as they will contain sensitive personal information.

When reviewing the application follow your broker's or company's guidelines. When we review an application there isn't actually an exact result that must be met for approval, such as credit score, etc. I have seen people who have terrible credit but they make plenty of money. Usually this is the result of a divorce or some other special circumstance, and we will take that into consideration. The one guideline that is not flexible is regarding income. Our office policy is that the applicant must show 3x (times) the monthly rent. If the apartment is $1200 per month, they must show $3600 in gross income for the month. Any less than that and you could run into trouble. You may have the nicest, most well intentioned tenant but if they simply don't make enough money, they won't be able to pay the bills. So save them and yourself the trouble and stick to the income guidelines. Because we are dealing with people and everyone's life is different, you will come across a myriad of backgrounds. Use your best judgement and go with your gut. If they were a pushy and demanding and had a bad attitude during the application process you can pretty much bet it's only going to get worse once they move in. Luckily being a jerk is not a protected class and there's nothing that says you can't deny someone just because you don't like them. Go right ahead. You as the manager will have to deal with this person on an ongoing basis. So if you don't have a good feeling about them, that's ok - go with your initial gut reaction. Follow up with previous landlords and get a feel for them as well. If there are still some things in the background info that doesn't seem right, set up a phone or face to face follow-up interview with the applicant and ask them directly about any discrepancies and make a judgement call. If you feel good about them and the income matches up, take all other things into consideration. We normally don't accept anyone who's had a recent eviction either. However, I remember one woman who had been evicted about 3 years prior. She explained to me the situation, said that she had gotten her life together since and went to nursing school and turned it all around. Her income was solid and was even able to get her work supervisor to co-sign for her. I liked her a lot as a person and so we decided to take a chance and she worked out great. Remember there are always certain laws and guidelines that must be followed. But, this is a people business and you will have to sometimes put things into perspective and just do what you think is right when it comes to approving a tenant's application.

Summary:

- Ask the right questions during your initial contact.
- Set up showings to effectively manage your time and effort.
- Collect and process the application using fees and strict company guidelines.
- Always be sure to follow fair housing laws and never discriminate.

CHAPTER 7 -
WORKING WITH
AFFORDABLE
HOUSING AGENCIES

* * *

If you choose to work with affordable housing agencies, often called Section-8 or HUD housing, there are some pros and cons that you should be aware of before doing so. I worked for several years with an agency that specializes in Section-8 housing. I will give my opinion on what those advantages and disadvantages are and how to best mitigate any potential risks that could arise.

I have worked with owners that love section-8 and end up wanting to make it a part of their main overall investing strategy, and I have worked with owners who end up hating the program and swear that they will never again participate in it. I can completely understand both points of view.

Let's cover first the main advantages of the HUD affordable housing programs. The biggest and most obvious advantage is that the rent is guaranteed. I say that with an asterisk added because nothing is guaranteed. But what that really means is that every month, right on time you will receive your rent payment, or at least most of it. The tenant may or may not have to contribute a portion of the overall rent depending on their financial situation. However for the most part, the rent is paid. Another advantage is that there is tremendous demand right now. You will not have any trouble finding someone who needs an affordable unit. In the county in Florida from which we operate there is actually a waiting list. It was not uncommon for the housing agency to call us directly and ask if we had any available units coming up. If you read the news and are in touch with the industry you'll know that there is a shortage of affordable housing in the country right now. So demand is certainly strong. Another advantage is that the rental rate that is provided is very competitive. Many people think that they won't receive market rents, and this is not true. In many cases we would receive above what we may have otherwise been able to get in a straight-pay situation.

Those are the main advantages of working the affordable housing programs. But as with any government agency, there is going to be situations where you are held down by red-tape and slow bureaucratic processes. The main disadvantages of working with HUD housing programs is that you are no longer the one in control of your rental property. You give up some of that control when you enter the program.

When you decide to accept a section 8 resident, you will first have to go through a HUD inspection. Make sure that your property will pass the inspections the first time around. Otherwise your timeline can be severely delayed as you have to go back and fix any deficiencies they find and then file a request for re-inspection. I have seen tenants who expect to be moving in on a certain date only to find out the unit didn't pass inspection and they end up getting delayed a month or more in extreme cases. I have literally seen people become homeless due to the backlog of the housing agencies. So, don't let this happen. Also your unit will be sitting vacant and you won't be getting paid during this time. HUD provides a list of all the items that will be inspected before approval, so make sure you have everything set before your inspection.

After the tenant moves in, the house will need to be maintained to this HUD standard. We always prided ourselves in going above and beyond the basic requirements and always did our best to provide quality housing for our residents. But you must remember that there will be times in which the housing agency tells you what needs to be done in a given situation. They are the ones who are in control. If you have a resident that knows how to take advantage of this relationship you can be in for a lot more work than it may be worth. I remember one time we had a tenant who knew the game very well and would play both sides of the situation. When it comes to accepting payment from a housing agency you must follow certain guidelines. Part of those guidelines are that the house must at all times remain in compliance with the HUD standards. If something in the house were to break down or an issue were to arise that would affect these standards, the repairs must be made right away. Most of the time, if something goes wrong, the tenant will call you directly and let you know there's an issue. In cases where you have a landlord who is not making the repairs they're supposed to, a recourse for the tenant is to call the housing agency and inform them of the problem. At this point the housing agency would send out an inspector to verify the issue and then send a letter informing the landlord that they must fix the issue by a certain deadline. This policy is in place to keep the property owners and managers in line and to ensure the house is in good standing. If the repairs aren't made by the date of the deadline the housing agency can do what's called, "abatement." Abatement is when they suspend all rent and will not pay you any monies until the deficiencies are fixed. Abated rent is gone forever. You will not get any of that money back and the process to have it reinstated can take weeks. Also, if the tenant has a portion of rent to pay, they are not responsible for paying anything during this time.

We once had a tenant that was responsible for paying a large portion of the rent, over 70% of the overall rate. He didn't like this and decided that he was going to play some games. I remember we received a deficiency notice from housing that there was an issue with this person's house. "That's strange" I remember thinking, he didn't call me to tell me about it. Ok no problem - we immediately tasked maintenance to take care of it. Fast forward a few weeks and we get an abatement notice! Not good! How could this have happened? Long story short, what we found out was that he was telling the housing inspector one thing, and then when our maintenance person showed up for the repair, he told him it was something else. He was able to do this because the inspection report was vauge, It simply said, repair rotted wood. Well he had found some rotted wood in two areas of the house. So he showed the HUD inspector one area and showed our maintenance person a different area. Then when the inspector came back he showed him the original spot and claimed we never came out to fix it. Bam, abatement. Eventually we figured it out and got control of the situation. It also exposed some flaws in our communication system at the time, so in hindsight it was a good thing. But it did go to show that you have to be careful when you are dealing with the housing agencies, they are there for the benefit of the tenant, not you as the landlord.

Now this is a rather extreme case. I have dealt with hundreds of HUD assisted units and most people don't behave this way. They are great people who are happy to have quality housing they can afford. Just remember though, you are beholden to a 3rd party government agency to which you are giving up some control in exchange for guaranteed rent monies. Just decide if it's the right situation for you and your owner.

Summary:
- Working with Section 8 has pros and cons.
- Be sure you keep your properties in good condition.
- Be sure communication between all parties is clear.

- Understand the process and decide if it's a good fit for your owner and their property.

CHAPTER 8 - COMPLETING THE LEASE & MOVING IN

* * *

OK, we've come a long way, but we're not quite there yet! So far you have learned what property management is and what the main responsibilities of the property manager are. You have learned how to market yourself and your services on the internet. From that marketing you have been able to generate leads of new clients and have been able to contract with them to manage their home or investment property. You have prepared and advertised the units, done showings and screened the applicants, and now you now have a qualified applicant and are ready to complete the lease and get them moved in. Great job, you're almost there.

However, completing the lease and performing a move-in inspection is a very important step and you want to make sure that at this point, all the expectations are clear and that all the paperwork is done completely and properly. When it comes to completing the lease, you want to make sure you are using a lease that is specific to your state, and is also approved by your broker. If you are doing management independently I highly recommend hiring an attorney to help you. There are a ton of websites and boilerplate leases available on the internet. I don't recommend using any of these. If you are new to property management there will be situations and scenarios that you won't see coming. If there is not a clause in the lease that addresses that situation, it's too late after the fact. So make sure you are using the lease that is approved by your broker or one that has been created by an attorney who is familiar and experienced in property management and landlord tenant laws, as well as fair housing laws. You also want to avoid ever being accused of practicing law without a license. So never use an "internet" lease or one that is not approved by your broker or real estate attorney.

More and more common today is the method of e-sign or electronic signatures for completing leases. Many of the popular management software systems will offer an e-sign feature. There are also other products like DocuSign and the like that will allow you to have your tenants complete the lease and other documents over email or even their tablet or phone. This can be very convenient for everyone and can save lots of time. However, I feel that it's very important at the time of signing a lease that your tenant has all their questions answered and most importantly that all the expectations are set. Make sure that not only is the lease complete but that the important parts, which are things that the tenant may be responsible for on an on going basis are highlighted and covered and understood. The last thing you want to hear tenants say is, "I didn't know I was responsible for that…"

All leases will tend to have some boilerplate legalese, and whether you decide to complete your leases in person or electronically, make sure your tenants are clear on the "important parts". These are the things that they will be directly responsible for on an ongoing basis. What I like to do is present the tenants with a summary sheet of the important highlights. This is a one-page form that simply outlines some of these points. It will have several one or two sentence lines with a checkbox or place for the tenant to initial each point indicating they understand along with reference to where the item can be found in the lease. For example one of these bullet points may be things like;

- Tenant responsible for maintaining lawn and landscaping (section 2.1 paragraph 3)
- Tenant responsible for all utilities including electric, water (section 3.6 paragraph 2)
- Tenant responsible for changing air filters every 30 days (etc, etc,..)

You can customize the highlight sheet as needed but I have always found that it's a good and simple way to get the tenant to acknowledge what their main responsibilities are throughout the tenancy. Have them initial each item and sign and date the form as well. You can present them with this at the time the lease is signed or beforehand so that they are clear on what's expected of them. You can also do it during the initial move-in or walkthrough inspection. It will help reiterate the main points you want them to know about.

Collecting rents and deposits. When it comes to collecting the monies, make sure you are following the law and the instructions of your owner and broker. For security deposits, they must be held in a trust account and never commingled with other funds. Also, most states require that the security deposit never exceed an amount equal to one month's rent. Always refer to your attorney and broker on these matters. The one thing I do want to comment on is again in regards to technology. Nowadays most people want to pay electronically and online. This is a great way to go. If your office is set up for it, collecting rents and deposits electronically can be a big time saver and it keeps you from having to physically handle the funds and provides an electronic "paper trail," which will help alleviate any confusion on when and where the monies were received. After all rent and deposits are paid, next is to do a walkthrough inspection with your tenants.

Performing a walkthrough inspection and condition of property report upon move-in is paramount. This will be a very important step and an invaluable set of forms that you will keep with your property files. You don't want there to be any disagreements when it comes time for the tenant to move out and you are making a claim on the security deposit for something that's broken and damaged just to hear the tenants claim that it was already like that when they moved in. Without a completed walkthrough inspection report it may be your word against theirs. But with a signed condition of property report, there will be no way for the tenant to make that claim after the fact.

Performing a walkthrough inspection is simple and there are plenty of generic forms like these on the internet. I would say it's fine to use this kind of boilerplate "internet" form. Just make sure it's approved by your broker or attorney. But, what's most important is making sure that it details each room and area of the house or apartment and allows for the tenant to sign off on the fact that everything is in good condition. Even if there is a small issue like a scratch here, or a dent there, it just needs to be noted. It's not necessarily something that would need to be fixed right away, but simply a record of condition stating what is. If you have ever rented a car, they take you around the car before you drive off and note any dents or dings, and then have you sign off on the forms. The move-in inspection is very much the same sort of thing. It's just a record for your files.

There is also a few new products on the market that, like the e-sign lease, will allow you to complete the property condition reports electronically. Some of the popular management software solutions offer it as an integrated/upgrade to their service and there are also stand alone features as well. There is one in particular that has the tenant go through the house using their phone. It acts like a DocuSign for images requiring the tenant to check off on each room and make notes about the condition. This can be very effective and time-saving. Just make sure that it gets completed. When possible, I like to personally do a walkthrough with the tenants. It allows them to ask questions and puts more of a personal touch on things. There's also less chance that something is missed when done in person. I am all about using technology to save time and effort, but just make sure that corners are being cut in the name of efficiency.

OK, you have had your tenants complete the lease and walk-through inspection. You've collected all your rents and deposits per the lease agreement and, you've answered all their questions and they are moved in. Congratulations. You are well on your way to being a successful property manager. However, unlike a real estate sales transaction where you may go years at a time without interacting with your clients again. Management is an ongoing relationship. The next chapter will discuss how to maintain those relationships and ensure you are successful for the long haul. Building your portfolio of rental properties will be the key to success.

Summary:

- Be sure to use lease agreements that are approved by your broker or attorney.
- Make sure your tenants are aware of their responsibilities under the lease terms.
- Use a one page highlight sheet to ensure understanding.
- Perform a walkthrough inspection and have the tenants complete a property condition report.

CHAPTER 9 - MANAGING FOR THE LONG TERM BY BUILDING RELATIONSHIPS

* * *

Congrats on getting this far. If you have followed the advice in this book hopefully you have been able to market yourself, find some clients, advertise their units find and screen tenants and get them to commit to a lease and moved them in. If you are still working on it and don't have any clients yet, that's ok too. Keep at it and you will have success.

Property management is about building long term relationships. I hold 2 broker licenses and have worked in several brokerages throughout the years. Sales and property management are different. While they both have similar characteristics and having experience in real estate sales will help you. But there are differences. Not to say that you shouldn't develop long term relationships with your sales clients, you absolutely should. The top producers do just that. They make sure they keep in touch with their clients over the years so the next time it's time to buy or sell, they can be there to serve those clients.

But when it comes to property management, you will be communicating with your owners and tenants on a very frequent basis. I'm not saying you have to speak with the same folks everyday. But it will be at least once a month. Possibly more depending on what's going on with the property. This is mostly in regards to owners, rather than tenants. Some tenants don't need too much attention. If the house is in good shape and they pay on time and are responsible, several months can go by without any communication at all. We try not to let more than 90 days pass without any contact though. It's important to remind the tenants that you are there and to be sure to have them communicate any issues with the house. Sometimes you will have tenants who don't speak up when they should. They let an issue go on for too long and that's not a good thing either. So make sure you are connecting at least on a quarterly basis.

Connecting and communicating with owners however, is your most important duty. You are there as the representative of the owner, and you are in charge of ensuring the property is kept in order. But it's not enough to just do what you're supposed to do and leave it at that.

As a manager, you are the eyes and ears for the owner and they want to see and hear from you. The biggest trap that most property managers fall into is not connecting with the owner when things are going well. It's easy to be in contact when there are issues going on that require communicating. But it's the times when there's not much to report that people can forget to keep in touch. In our office we have a policy that every owner needs to hear from their property manager at least once a month. Just check in with an email or a phone call and say, "Hey, Mr or Mrs owner, I just wanted to touch base with you and let you know that everything is going great with your property. The tenant has paid on time and there aren't any maintenance issues at this time..." Etc.

It's also a good idea to provide them with a calendar of events such as upcoming inspections, or lease renewal dates or routine maintenance tasks. It helps keep them in the loop and shows them that you are on top of things. This will provide owners with piece of mind. Most owners just want to hear from someone and be told that everything is ok. If you remember the story I told at the beginning of this book about the terrible property management experience I had. This was one of the (many) issues I had with them. No one ever called me or communicated anything with me. I'd have to call and text and email and hope to get a timely response. It was stressful and led to nothing but animosity in the relationship. It was a horrible experience and I would never recommend that company to anyone. That's not the way you want to be remembered.

When it comes to your owners, and tenants, make sure you are being the type of person that they would speak highly of. Be the person who goes out of their way to make sure things get done. Go above and beyond and people will recommend you to others. Most people feel that the tenant and landlord often have an antagonistic relationship, but I find this to actually be the exception rather than the rule. We focus on good communication and treating people with respect and kindness at all times, no matter who they are or what the situation is.

I had been managing a multi-family property for an owner one time and everything was going well. But one day he called up and said that he had decided not to renew the management agreement. He said that he was moving back to the area and wanted to manage it himself. OK, no problem I told him. Then some time went by and he called me up asking if I could help. He wanted me to help him find and screen tenants. Because we parted on good terms and we always did right by him, he trusted us. So when he needed real estate services in the future he called us. I have since helped him find and place a number of tenants for his units. Even though we didn't have an on-going service agreement for the management, he still wanted to use our services because he knew that we would do a good job of marketing the units and screening the tenants.

There are also times in property management where you will have the opportunity to be a hero. There will often be cases in which the owner is hiring you because they've been burned by another management company and you will be in a position to help turn things around and save the day. Just be aware that these owners will be a little sensitive and probably somewhat untrusing of property managers in the beginning. Do the things we've discussed in this book and you will soon have the property turned around.

One time we took on a property of about 20 units. The owners were not local and they feared that the original management company was letting things slip. They had enjoyed some solid income for a while but all of a sudden they weren't getting the income they used to and they noticed other issues as well. So they decided to let that management company go and hire us. The old managers were not happy and it was not a friendly handover. They provided us with no information and left us in the dark to figure it all out. Once the smoke had cleared, we discovered that of the 20 units - only 3 were performing. The owners were pissed! They had no idea how bad it was and we had to be the messengers who brought the bad news. It took a long time to get things turned around. But we had developed a solid plan, worked hard and always kept the interests of the owners front and center. After many months we finally got their property cash flowing again and we were heroes. If you can do this for an owner you will have a loyal client for life.

Another time recently we faced a situation we had never faced before. Someone called us and said that they were going to cancel their management contract because things were going so well!

Like so often is the case, they had hired us to turn around their rental units after having gone through some bad renters and they were facing long vacancies from inaction.They had self-managed from a long distance and things had slowly fallen apart on them until one day it just all came to a head. We took over and were able to fill all their vacancies with stellar tenants in record time. Now the units are performing so well and the tenants are so good they started entertaining the idea of canceling the management agreement and taking back over themselves. But after a short discussion reminding them of how they got into the situation of high vacancies and low collections to begin with, they quickly changed their tune and decided to keep us as their management company.

When it comes to property management, there will always be some event or person that can be difficult to deal with. However, it can also be very rewarding. When done right it will provide you with a profitable and satisfying career. You can develop some wonderful relationships and become more involved in the community.

Recently we were chosen to work with some of the biggest representatives of the local housing authority to participate in a program that would help eliminate homelessness for families with children within the city. It has been a very rewarding experience and we are honored to be a part of the program. But to go far in the industry, you will need to educate yourself and continue your education beyond basic CE requirements from your state or real estate board. It will be your responsibility to raise the level of your game. Most people will not take the time to do this. Since you are reading this book, you are clearly interested in improving your property management skills. You are already ahead of the crowd.

Summary:
- Keep in touch with your owners and tenants on a regular basis

- Maintain good communication
- Always provide the best service you can

CHAPTER 10 - CONCLUSION. JUST THE BEGINNING

* * *

While you have just completed this short book on how to get started in property management, the journey is only just beginning. Only you will be able to get out there and take action. You will be responsible for making the career you want to have. Since you've just read a book on property management, it's likely you are interested in the field of property management. Which like all real estate, can have very defined specialities. You will want to choose a property type and attempt to specialize in it. Become the expert, so that when people need service in your specialty, they know to call you.

This book offers a general look at mostly residential property management. But there are many different property types and almost all of them can benefit from the services of a good property management company. Decide what property type you want to be involved in and get started today.

When it comes to finding your niche. Go with what you like. There are different types of property managers depending on the type of property. Each property type will require a special set of skills and a specialized knowledge in order to effectively manage it. It will be important that whatever property type you decide to manage you educate yourself on the in's and out's of how to effectively operate and manage that particular property. If you don't have experience one way to get some hands on training is to find someone in that field who is already successful and where you want to be and find out what you can do for them. Most people will be willing to help you if you offer to bring them value first.

Residential - Residential property management will be the main focus of this book. It is the field in which I have the most knowledge and experience. Many of the examples and scenarios in this book come from the perspective of a residential property manager. Residential management and leasing is probably the most common and most easily understood of all the property management specialties. It's likely that we have all been involved in residential property management one way or another. Let's say you have just rented your first apartment. You were still involved in the property management and residential leasing business whether you realized it or not. Someone had to show you the unit and provide you with a lease. Depending on the size of the property it may have been a manager or it may just have been the owner themselves. You probably completed an application, signed a lease and paid rent and deposits. Even if you had never thought about it from the perspective of the management side, you were still involved in residential leasing. You just happened to be the tenant/resident in this case.

It's because of this familiarity of residential leasing that makes it an easy place to start for the aspiring property manager. There is a basic understanding of how the process works. However, as you hopefully discovered by reading this book, there is a lot more to know than just how to show an apartment and sign a lease. Those activities tend to simply be the final result of all the hard work you did upfront. Showing the apartment to qualified applicants and singing the lease are the results of your hard work.

HOA/ Association Management - HOA and association management can be quite different than managing a small apartment building. Certain states may require additional licensing in order to manage an HOA. There are often differences in the fee structure as compared to other types of property management. Many HOA management firms specialize only in community management. If this is of interest to you, find someone who is successful in the field and learn all you can from them. Get the necessary licensing and dedicate to the speciality. It can be a very rewarding management path.

Commercial Real Estate Management - Commercial Real estate can be quite different than residential. While there is residential real estate that is considered commercial real estate, most commercial real estate is not considered residential. Commercial real estate is often the term that is used to refer to all income property that is not residential. Most often, commercial real estate is considered to be more like retail and office space, properties like shopping centers, malls, outlet stores, etc. All these types of properties are generally considered to be commercial real estate. The fact is that there are many variations of commercial real estate such as the sub-groups of the types listed above.

Facility Management - Facility management is a broad term and type of property management that can require some specialized knowledge. It is unlikely that a single agent or even a small management firm would handle the operations and management of a facility. Of course, there are always exceptions, and depending on the size and type and definition of facility, the complexities, duties and required knowledge will vary greatly. Facility management more commonly refers to larger properties with lots of moving parts and operations.

Choosing where to begin - what kind of property management will you choose? What kind of property types are you interested in? In the beginning it will be most wise for you to try a few different areas of management until you find the one that suits you. You can help other agents in the fields you're interested in, in exchange for knowledge or hands on experience in that field of management or property type. Get a feel for the property types you like and get involved in any way you can.

Many agents think that they will just take any management account that comes their way. While this may be tempting, it may not necessarily be the smart thing to do. I realize that if you are just starting out in PM, the idea of turning down any accounts sounds like a bad idea. But when it comes to property management, you will be communicating and reporting to your owners quite often throughout the year. It will be important that you are able to perform your job properly and that you know what's involved. If you have only ever managed apartments and houses do not try to manage warehouses or office buildings without some experience and knowledge in these areas. I do realize however that many of you reading this book may be at the early stages of your property management career and that you may not have a lot of experience. Hopefully this book will give you a good foundation with which to work. You would be surprised how often people are willing to help, if you just ask for the help. Most high quality professionals love the opportunity to help others succeed. They don't have a mentality of scarcity. They believe there is enough to go around for everyone. At least for those who are willing to put in the time to learn and put in the work and effort required.

If you'd like to connect with me reach out on LinkedIn, or contact me through my blog at; https://PropertyManagementPete.com. I'm always happy to hear from people who have questions or comments regarding property management. If you're in the Tampa Bay area come join us at one of our Ultimate Landlord meetups or stop by our office in St Petersburg, FL. We're happy to meet with you!

Thanks for reading! Best of luck in your property management career.

Sincerely,

- Pete Garian
"Property Management Pete"

.

www.ingramcontent.com/pod-product-compliance
Lightning Source LLC
Chambersburg PA
CBHW041103180526
45172CB00001B/90